NICO

FRYE ART MUSEUM

NICOLAI FECHIN

EDITED BY JO-ANNE BIRNIE DANZKER

FRYE ART MUSEUM

	6	Foreword
Jo-Anne Birnie Danzker	12	International Success: 1909–1914
	27	War and Revolution in Russia: 1914–1922
	33	New York: 1923–1927
Lauren Palmor	42	Taos and California: 1927–1955
	71	Biography
	75	Notes

FOREWORD

One hundred years after Nicolai Fechin (1881–1955) burst onto the international scene with a "barbaric mastery of form and color,"[1] an international alliance of museums and private individuals under the aegis of the Foundation for International Arts and Education (FIAE) is celebrating his exceptional accomplishments in a series of exhibitions in cities as far afield as Kazan, Russia; Saint Petersburg; Moscow; Minneapolis, Minnesota; and now Seattle. These exhibitions, made possible by the strong support of the State Museum and Exhibition Center ROSIZO under the auspices of the Ministry of Culture of the Russian Federation, were initiated by the founder of FIAE, the late Gregory Guroff.

The exhibition at the Frye Art Museum in Seattle brings together paintings and drawings from its extensive holdings of Fechin's work with canvases from American museums and private lenders in both the Russian Federation and the United States. Among them are paintings that established Fechin's reputation in the United States, including *Lady in Pink (Portrait of Natalia Podbelskaya)*, 1912, today a highlight of the collection of the Frye Art Museum. One of Fechin's finest works, this canvas was exhibited in the Annual Exhibition at the Carnegie Institute in Pittsburgh, Pennsylvania, in 1913 and the Panama-Pacific International Exposition in San Francisco in 1915.

The Frye Art Museum initiated a retrospective survey dedicated to Fechin's accomplishments in 2009, exactly thirty-three years after mounting a major exhibition of his paintings with loans from institutions across the Soviet Union. We wished to examine the role Fechin had played not only in Russia, Europe, and the United States but also in China, where reproductions of his paintings and drawings became a mainstay of academic training for artists. In the process of preparing this exhibition, we learned that a large-scale exhibition of Fechin's paintings would be touring the Russian Federation in 2011–2012 under the auspices of ROSIZO and FIAE. Our Board of Trustees agreed to lend key paintings by Fechin from our collection to all venues of this important project, to ensure that his career in both Russia and the United States could be properly recognized, and the Frye Art Museum became part of this initiative.

We wish to express our deep appreciation to Greg, Kathie, and Alec Guroff of FIAE for their efforts in bringing this highly complex project to fruition despite at times intractable complications. Our ability to present Fechin's accomplishments in both his Russian and American periods has been made possible by the generous support of museums across the United States and private lenders in both Russia and the United States (acknowledged on page 9). We are deeply indebted to them. We also wish to recognize the support of ROSIZO in securing loans from the Russian Federation; they themselves have been supported in their efforts on behalf of the Frye Art Museum by Rosgosstrakh (RGS) Group of Companies and Alexander Dadiani.

The Seattle exhibition and this publication are funded by the Frye Foundation and Frye Art Museum members and donors and are made possible by the generous support of the Filatov Family Art Foundation and BNY Mellon Wealth Management. Seasonal support of the Frye Art Museum is provided by 4Culture, Seattle Office of Arts and Cultural Affairs, Canonicus Fund, and ArtsFund.

I would like to express my personal gratitude to Galina Tuluzakova, formerly of the State Museum of Fine Arts of the Republic of Tatarstan, who has dedicated the greater part of her professional life to researching the life and work of Nicolai Fechin. As curator of the retrospective exhibition that toured the Russian Federation, and author of a number of volumes on Fechin, she has been an important resource for us.

I would like to acknowledge at the Frye Art Museum Lauren Palmor, Research Assistant, Collections & Exhibitions, who provided invaluable support in researching the American period of Fechin's career; Scott Lawrimore, Deputy Director, Collections & Exhibitions; Cory Gooch, Collections Manager/Registrar; and Shane Montgomery, Exhibition Designer, and his team, for their exceptional contribution to all aspects of our exhibition, from conservation of the works to final installation. I would like to thank Amelia Hooning, Assistant, Exhibitions & Publications, for coordination of the exhibition and catalogue. In conclusion, I would like to acknowledge Jeffrey Hirsch, Deputy Director, Communications, and Victoria Culver, Senior Designer, whose dedication and skill made this publication possible.

Jo-Anne Birnie Danzker
Director, Frye Art Museum

FOREWORD

The Foundation for International Arts and Education is pleased to join the Frye Art Museum in presenting this important exhibition dedicated to Nicolai Fechin. Despite political obstacles during its inception, it is a singular example of the dramatic impact cultural exchange can have in expanding the world for museum visitors in both countries. Visitors to the exhibition and readers of this catalogue will be able to appreciate the unique cultural heritage Russia and the United States have gained through the creative contributions of Nicolai Fechin.

In Saint Petersburg in 2003, visitors to an exhibition of American landscapes and portraits of Native Americans were instantly drawn to a single work, *Joe with Drum*. Fascinated by the exotic foreign subject, they instantly recognized the artistic style as belonging to one of their own—Nicolai Fechin. This unexpected connection provided the impetus for a major project exploring the impact of Russian émigrés on American culture. That project culminated in a multiyear exhibition, *American Artists from the Russian Empire,* in which American audiences learned about the background of artists seen as truly "American," and Russian audiences gained an appreciation for the work of their émigré compatriots who had become integral members of their adopted culture.

This exhibition in Seattle is testament to private initiative and cultural collaboration. It provides a broader context for the Frye's major collection of Fechin's work and presents a showcase for a new era of Russian collectors. Catherine the Great bought vast collections for her palaces; the Shchukins and Morozovs were preeminent contemporary collectors of the Impressionists. Today, Russian collectors such as the Filatov Family Art Foundation have contributed substantial resources to revealing the breadth and depth of Russia's cultural heritage to a wider audience and showcasing this rich legacy for museum visitors abroad. The same commitment is manifested by multiple private Russian collectors who have stepped up to support the American venues of the Fechin exhibition. Without the dedication of the Frye staff, the generous support of these collectors, and a little ingenuity, it would have been nearly impossible to present such an excellent retrospective of Nicolai Fechin.

Alec Guroff
President, Foundation for International Arts and Education

LENDERS TO THE EXHIBITION

The Eugene B. Adkins Collection at the Fred Jones Jr. Museum of Art, the University of Oklahoma, Norman, Oklahoma, and the Philbrook Museum of Art, Tulsa, Oklahoma

The Vladimir Berezovsky Collection, Saint Petersburg

The Dr. and Mrs. Charles R. Briggs Collection

The Filatov Family Art Foundation

Kournikova Gallery, Moscow

The Kirill Naumov Collection, Saint Petersburg

The New Mexico Museum of Art

Panhandle-Plains Historical Museum, Canyon, Texas, Johnie Griffin Collection

Panhandle-Plains Historical Museum, Canyon, Texas, James D. Hamlin Collection

Gerald Peters Gallery, Santa Fe, New Mexico

Private collection, ID

Private collection, Russia

Private collection, USA

Private Collection of Tia

The San Diego Museum of Art

The Sepherot Foundation Collection, Liechtenstein

Stark Museum of Art, Orange, Texas

The Gil Waldman Collection

Fechin premiered his masterpiece *Lady in Pink* at the 1913 Annual Exhibition at the Carnegie Institute, where it was presented in the same room as *Salome*, 1906, by the cofounder of the Munich Secession, Franz von Stuck. Two years later, *Lady in Pink* was showcased in the Panama-Pacific International Exposition in San Francisco together with the work of Pierre Puvis de Chavannes, Claude Monet, Camille Pissarro, Pierre-Auguste Renoir, and Alfred Sisley. In 1915, an enthusiastic Eugen Neuhaus described *Lady in Pink* as displaying "a very unusual virtuosity," explaining that "the handling of paint in this canvas is most extraordinary, possessing a technical quality few other canvases in the entire exhibition have. There is life, such as very few painters ever attain, and seen only in the work of a master. . . . I have a strange fondness for this weird canvas."[a] In 1919, the painting was included in the First Annual Exhibition of Contemporary International Art in Dallas. It was exhibited together with *Portrait of a Young Woman* (p. 31) at the *Exhibition of Russian Painting and Sculpture* at the Brooklyn Museum and in Fechin's solo exhibition at the Art Institute of Chicago, both in 1923.

Lady in Pink (Portrait of Natalia Podbelskaya), 1912
Oil on canvas
45 1/2 x 35 in. (115.57 x 88.9 cm)
Frye Art Museum, 1990.005

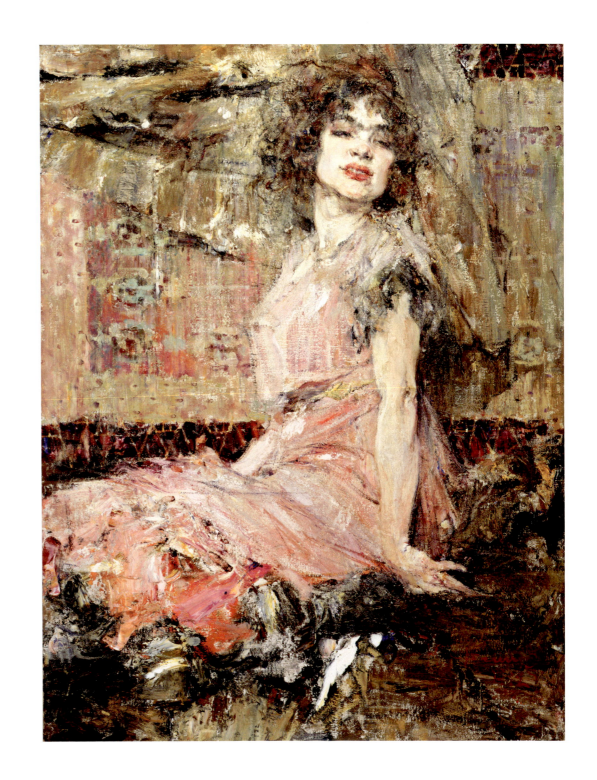

JO-ANNE BIRNIE DANZKER   INTERNATIONAL SUCCESS: 1909–1914

The canvas of thirty-year-old Russian artist Nicolai Fechin (1881–1955) that had the place of honor in the Vanderbilt Gallery of the National Academy of Design, New York, in December 1911 was described as savage, splendid, and heterogeneous in *The Craftsman*. Its placement near an "aesthetic" portrait by American artist William Merritt Chase (1849–1916) made Fechin's "barbaric mastery of form and color" all the more convincing to the admiring critic, while Chase appeared by comparison to be "ultra-modern" and American.[1] Fechin's canvas, *L'enlèvement d'une nouvelle mariée* (Bearing Off the Bride),[2] depicts a traditional wedding ritual among the Cheremis or Mari tribes near Kazan, Tatarstan, where the artist was born.[3] *American Art News* also urged art lovers to visit the Sixth Annual Winter Exhibition of the Academy to see what it described as a clever, remarkable, unusual, and important canvas "by the noted Russian painter." It agreed that the painting deserved its place of honor and observed that it had been lent by the prominent New York merchant and art collector George A. Hearn.[4] Fechin, it noted, "is a master of technique and a diligent sociological student."[5] While F.J.M. Jr., writing in the *Nation,* agreed that the painting was unquestionably among the most striking contributions to the National Academy's exhibition, he nevertheless expressed reservations: "Fechin has plenty of the disorderly power befitting his race. His peasant rout is painted with gusto, but there is no unity beyond that of subject matter."[6] While there was no unanimity regarding Fechin's "disorderly" mastery of color and paint, consensus remained that this was a "star" canvas.[7]

The discussion of *Bearing Off the Bride* in December 1911 and the recognition of Fechin as an artist of note are remarkable in that he had exhibited in the United States only twice before, at the Annual Exhibition at the Carnegie Institute in Pittsburgh, in the summers of 1910 and 1911. In his debut at the Carnegie, Fechin presented depictions of key personages in his artistic and familial life: *Portrait of Miss Sapojnikoff*, 1908 (p. 13), and *Portrait of My Father*.[8] Both contrasted sharply with the perfectly finished portraits prevalent in the salons of Pittsburgh and New York at that time. *Art and Progress* described *Portrait of Miss Sapojnikoff* as "broadly painted and insistent with personality,"[9] while James B. Townsend noted in *American Art News* that "[t]he portrait of Mlle. Lapojnikof [Sapojnikoff] by Fechin has the most dexterous technique imaginable and throbs with vitality. The use of pigment in the brocaded apron is worth the journey to Pittsburgh to see and study."[10] The catalogue for the 1910 Carnegie exhibition noted that the young artist had received a number of awards, including medals from the Imperial Academy of Fine Arts and the Société des Beaux-Arts in Saint Petersburg. Mention was made of his first international success in 1909, at the joint Tenth International

Portrait of Miss Sapojnikoff, 1908
Oil on canvas
56 x 37 3/8 in. (142.2 x 94.9 cm)
The San Diego Museum of Art,
Gift of Mrs. John Burnham, 1964.141

Nadezha Mikhailovna Sapozhnikova, one of Fechin's earliest patrons, supported her fellow artists in Kazan by commissioning portraits, buying artworks, and donating to the scholarship fund of the School of Art. Fechin's portrait of Sapozhnikova was featured in his American debut at the 1910 Annual Exhibition at the Carnegie Institute in Pittsburgh. *Portrait of Miss Sapojnikoff* was acquired by prominent New York merchant and art collector George A. Hearn; upon Hearn's death, it was purchased by William S. Stimmel of Pittsburgh, who would later be instrumental in Fechin's emigration to the United States. In 1923, Fechin was represented in the landmark *Exhibition of Russian Painting and Sculpture* at the Brooklyn Museum with eighteen paintings, including *Portrait of Miss Sapojnikoff*, which was also included in a solo exhibition of his work at the Art Institute of Chicago that December.

Exhibition of the Munich Secession and Munich Künstlergenossenschaft (Artists' Association) in the city's prestigious Glass Palace. Here, in his debut exhibition outside Russia, Fechin was awarded a Medal, 2nd Class, for Painting,[11] not a gold medal as has been repeatedly suggested,[12] for an unidentified *Study* then in the possession of the Museum of the Imperial Academy of Fine Arts in Saint Petersburg.[13] Fechin's canvas was displayed along with those of leading Russian artists of the day, including his teacher Ilya Repin, Mikhail Nesterov (who was awarded a Medal, 1st Class), Nikolai Dubovskoi, Nicholas Roerich, and Valentin Serov.[14] The following year, in the summer of 1910, Fechin was invited to participate in the International Exhibition of the Munich Secession, where he exhibited *Bearing Off the Bride* and *Portrait Study*.[15]

By 1911, Fechin was a highly anticipated presence in international exhibitions in the United States, even if a disputed measure of a particular institution's "cosmopolitanism."[16] His contribution to the Carnegie's Annual Exhibition that year was an unidentified *Study* (a portrait of a child)[17] and the inimitable *Bearing Off the Bride*.[18] At the Russian Pavilion of the 1911 International Exposition in Rome he exhibited an unidentified *Study* owned by the Museum of the Imperial Academy of Fine Arts in Saint Petersburg, possibly the same canvas that had been exhibited in Munich the previous year.[19] Fechin's paintings were now eagerly sought by American collectors, in particular William S. Stimmel of Pittsburgh[20] and George A. Hearn[21] of New York, who each purchased one painting from the Carnegie exhibitions. Hearn acquired *Portrait of Miss Sapojnikoff* (p. 13) in 1910 and *Bearing Off the Bride* in 1911, while Stimmel acquired *Portrait of My Father* in 1910.[22] Given the limited number of canvases available for purchase from exhibitions in the United States, Stimmel and his business associate John R. Hunter, of Pittsburgh, began acquiring paintings directly from Fechin in Russia based on photographs the artist sent. Hunter's first such purchase was *Nude Figure*, 1911 (p. 29), which was followed by five additional acquisitions including *Portrait of a Young Woman*, 1912 (p. 31).[23] As a result, key masterworks associated with Fechin's Russian period (1909-23) were to be found in the United States rather than in Russia in the early twentieth century.[24]

Russian House, ca. 1910
Oil on canvas
14 3/8 x 15 5/8 in. (37.5 x 39.7 cm)
Private collection, USA

Russian Peasant Hut, ca. 1910
Oil on canvas
15 7/8 x 20 1/8 in. (40.32 x 51.12 cm)
Frye Art Museum, 1975.014

In 1912, Fechin was present at the Carnegie Institute's sixteenth Annual Exhibition with *Portrait of Kissa*,[25] described by one critic as an "engaging little portrait of a child with a doll."[26] This canvas failed to meet the high expectations of at least one of Fechin's early American admirers. The worthy Townsend, who had been so enamored of Fechin's *Portrait of Miss Sapojnikoff* (p. 13) in 1910, was disappointed that Fechin was

represented by "one small example only."²⁷ Nevertheless, *Portrait of Kissa* caught the attention of Christian Brinton (1870–1942), an internationally noted American critic, collector, and curator who would shape the reception of Fechin's work in the United States in the coming decade. In the British journal *International Studio*, Brinton wrote of seeing this work at the Annual Exhibition: "There is this year but one Russian canvas of note, the small *Portrait of Kissa* by Nicholas Fechin, yet in breadth of handling and searching grasp of character it dwarfs everything in its immediate vicinity."²⁸

Rustic House, ca. 1910
Mixed paint media on canvas
14 x 19 in. (35.56 x 48.26 cm)
Panhandle-Plains Historical Museum, Canyon, Texas, James D. Hamlin Collection, 832/1244

Young Boy, Russia '22, 1922
Charcoal on paper
17 x 14 3/4 in. (43.18 x 37.47 cm)
Frye Art Museum, 1977.008

Peasant Woman, Study to the "Cabbage Fest," 1909
Charcoal on laid paper
25 1/4 x 19 in. (64.14 x 48.26 cm)
Frye Art Museum, 1977.016

Study (for the painting "Shower"), ca. 1910
Oil on canvas
19 x 18 1/2 in. (48.5 x 47 cm)
The Vladimir Berezovsky Collection, Saint Petersburg

Completed during Fechin's final year at the Imperial Academy of Arts in Saint Petersburg, *Peasant Woman* served as a study for his canvas *Kapusnitza (The Cabbage Fest)*, which depicts a village celebration of a cabbage harvest. In 1909 Fechin enjoyed international success at the joint International Exhibition of the Munich Secession and Munich Künstlergenossenschaft (Artists' Association), exhibiting in the company of leading Russian artists of the day, including his teacher Ilya Repin, Nikolai Dubovskoi, and Valentin Serov. Fellow members of the Peredvizhniki artists' association (Wanderers or Itinerants), they were committed to art as a vehicle for social reform and national consciousness. The Russian landscape and peasantry were key themes in their paintings and in those of Fechin at this time.

Young Boy dates from 1922, a period of great deprivation in Russia, marked by disease, starvation, and loss of life. John R. Hunter recalled that when Fechin arrived in New York the following year, he had in his possession a number of fine charcoal drawings; it is possible that these were among them.

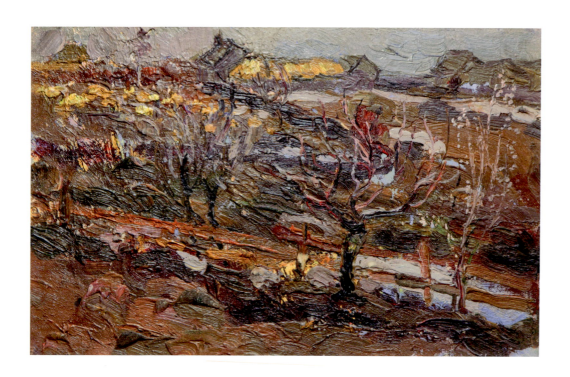

In the Evening, ca. 1910
Oil on canvas
9 7/8 x 13 3/4 in. (25 x 35 cm)
Private collection, Russia

Fechin's international success continued unabated in 1913 with the presentation of important paintings in Munich and Pittsburgh. In the joint Eleventh International Exhibition of the Munich Secession and Munich Künstlergenossenschaft, Fechin's *Portrait of Miss Podbelskaya*[29] was exhibited in the company of canvases by Ilya Repin and Nikolai Dubovskoi, fellow members of the Society for Traveling Art Exhibitions, a Russian artists' association. Known as Peredvizhniki, or Itinerants, these artists were committed to art as a vehicle for social reform and national consciousness. Key themes in their paintings as well as those of Fechin, the "diligent sociological student,"[30] were the Russian landscape and peasantry (pp. 14–18). At the 1913 Annual Exhibition at the Carnegie, Fechin thrilled American critics with a painting regarded as a masterpiece of the period, *Lady in Pink (Portrait of Natalia Podbelskaya)*, 1912 (p. 11), and *Portrait of Mlle. Kitaeve* (Portrait of

Miss Kitaeva) (p. 30), which would be purchased by the Minneapolis Society of Fine Arts.[31] Fechin's *Lady in Pink*, with her voluptuous red lips, half-closed eyes, and body dissolving in a virtuoso display of color and paint, provided a "modern" counterpart to *Salome*, 1906, the spectacular portrayal of eros and death by the cofounder of the Munich Secession, Franz von Stuck, which was exhibited in the same room.[32]

Fechin's presence on the international stage was only strengthened in 1914 when he was included in the inaugural exhibition of the Russian Pavilion at the prestigious Venice Biennale with compatriots such as Léon Bakst, Nikolai Dubovskoi, Nicholas Roerich, and Mikhail Vrubel. Fechin exhibited *Venditrice di cavoli* (Cabbage Seller),[33] possibly one of a series of works, such as the preparatory study of a peasant woman (p. 16), associated with his early canvas *Kapusnitza* (The Cabbage Fest). In 1914, Fechin was also included in the Annual Exhibition at the Carnegie Institute, this time with *Portrait in Sunlight*.[34] Townsend noted his presence in *American Art News*, writing, "That clever Russian Nicolas Fechin, whom Pittsburgh has made known to American art lovers, has two examples of his able brush—both portraits, one a half length, a study of a woman in white, marvelously clever in technique and splendid in expression."[35] The *Fine Arts Journal* drew an interesting comparison between the work of Fechin and Olga Boznańska (1865–1940), a distinguished Polish artist whose work was also on display in the Carnegie exhibition.[36] Both artists, it suggested, displayed a "common undercurrent of psychical feeling paramount in their work."[37] Seven decades later, the renowned scholar John Ellis Bowlt, in an essay on Symbolism and decadence in Russian art from 1890 to 1920, would propose that Fechin "favoured more grotesque subjects in the early 1900s."[38] He argued that Fechin and other prominent Russian artists of the period[39] employed caricature in a manner that displayed "an unwarranted measure" of distortion out of "a more expressionistic, psychological urge"[40] or even "prurient pleasure."[41] Fechin's finest works do display elements of the grotesque, an undercurrent of psychological intensity, and intense pleasure in pure expression. Exemplary early paintings in this exhibition include his 1910 study for *Shower* (p. 17) and portraits of Natalia Podbelskaya (p. 11) and Mademoiselle Girmond (p. 26). Indeed, throughout his entire career, across a wide range of subjects, and with increasing intensity,[42] Fechin conflated the grotesque, the psychological, and the sociological in virtuoso displays of paint and color. His use of pigment with very little oil, layers of color, and a dry brush technique that reveals the underlying canvas,[43] and his "disorderly" manner of representation that was simultaneously realistic and abstract, would find its true equivalents only decades later.

In his autobiography, Nicolai Fechin recalls that his father, Ivan Alexandrovitch Fechin, fostered his talents at an early age. A craftsman who specialized in making icons and carving altars, Ivan hoped that his son would one day assist him. The younger Fechin demonstrated a penchant for drawing, which he enjoyed after everyone else had gone to bed.

"The light from my lamp would annoy my father very much, since it naturally prevented him from sleeping. He would ask me, with tolerant politeness and forbearance, to go to bed. I would promise to do so but would immediately forget, being completely engrossed with my drawing. Finally he would lose patience, get out of bed, grab me by the scruff of the neck like a puppy, and dump me into my bed."[b]

In his American debut at the Carnegie Institute in 1910, Fechin presented a portrait of his father that contrasted sharply with the perfectly finished portraits prevalent in Pittsburgh salons at that time. It was acquired by William S. Stimmel, who lent it in 1923 to the *Exhibition of Russian Painting and Sculpture* at the Brooklyn Museum and to Fechin's solo exhibition at the Art Institute of Chicago.

Portrait of My Father, 1912
Oil on canvas
29 x 25 in. (73.66 x 63.5 cm)
The Eugene B. Adkins Collection at the Fred Jones Jr. Museum of Art, the University of Oklahoma, Norman, Oklahoma, and the Philbrook Museum of Art, Tulsa, Oklahoma

Portrait of Nina Belkovich, 1910
Oil on canvas
27 3/8 x 22 3/4 in. (69.5 x 57.8 cm)
Courtesy of Kournikova Gallery, Moscow

Fechin began his studies at the Kazan School of Art, which was cofounded in 1895 by Nicolai Belkovich, and completed them at the Imperial Academy of Arts in Saint Petersburg. On his return to Kazan to take up a teaching position at the School of Art in 1909, he developed a close friendship with Belkovich's daughter, Alexandra (1892–1983), who assisted him with his foreign correspondence and wrote letters in French to his collectors. This portrait from 1911 is one of the earliest of Alexandra, who was nineteen years old at the time. In 1913, the couple married, and the following year, their daughter, Eya (1914–2002), was born.

The portrait of Alexandra's cousin, Nina Vladimirovna Belkovich (1902–1983), was completed in 1910, the year Fechin participated for the first time in the Annual Exhibition at the Carnegie Institute in Pittsburgh. The following year, he exhibited an unidentified *Study* at the Carnegie, a "half length sketch portrait of a child."[c] An unidentified collector lent *Portrait of Nina Belkovich* to Fechin's solo exhibition at the Art Institute of Chicago in 1923, and it was illustrated in the catalogue under the title *Portrait (Study)*.[d]

Alexandra Belkovich, 1911
Oil on canvas
21 1/2 x 20 in. (54.6 x 50.8 cm)
The Eugene B. Adkins Collection at the
Fred Jones Jr. Museum of Art, the
University of Oklahoma, Norman,
Oklahoma, and the Philbrook Museum
of Art, Tulsa, Oklahoma

Portrait of Daughter Eya, ca. 1919–20
Oil on canvas
10 1/2 x 12 in. (26.67 x 30.48 cm)
The Kirill Naumov Collection,
Saint Petersburg

Christmas Tree, 1917
Oil on canvas
26 1/2 x 40 in. (67.3 x 101.6 cm)
The Vladimir Berezovsky Collection,
Saint Petersburg

In *Christmas Tree*, Fechin depicts Alexandra and their beloved three-year-old daughter, Eya, in the first year of the Russian Revolution. Alexandra had moved with Eya to the village of Vasilievo, twenty miles outside of Kazan, while Fechin remained in the city and taught at the School of Art. Alexandra recalled that, "of course like everyone else we lost everything entrusted to the city banks.... We turned most of the flower garden into a vegetable patch, placed several beehives in the raspberry beds and cleared the grounds along the brook for a cabbage and potato field."[e] Fechin visited Alexandra and Eya whenever he was able: "During the Revolution the family turned out to be the only haven where I could rest and revive my strength."[f] This peaceful idyll, however, could not be sustained. "Poor harvests. Starvation. Disease began to creep upon the banks of the Volga," Alexandra wrote. "Never before, nor since, have I experienced such tension in fighting for my own life and the life of those near me. Caught between the fearful waves of loosened human passions and the unconcern of nature, we had to turn ourselves to nature and pray for mercy."[g]

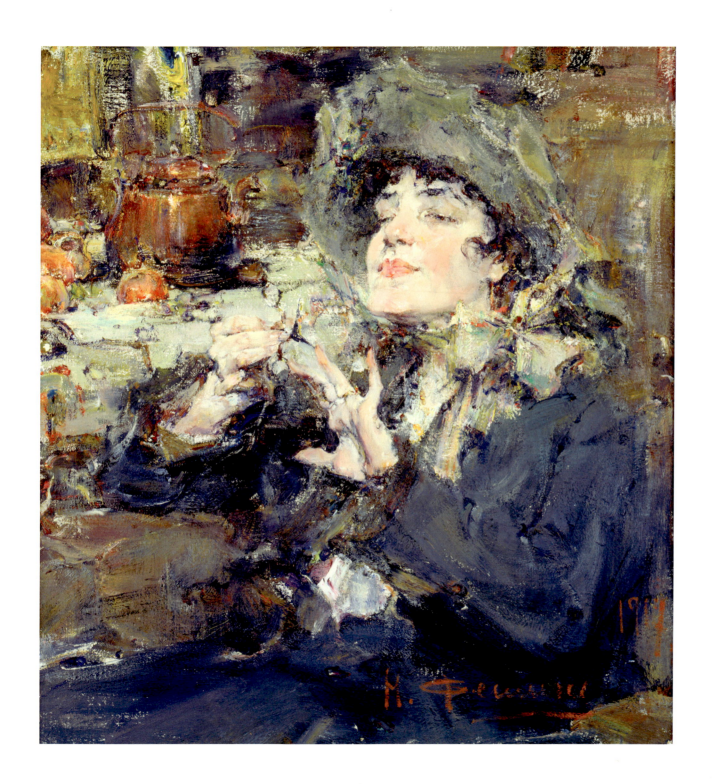

Manicure Lady (Portrait of Mademoiselle Girmond), 1917
Oil on canvas
28 1/8 x 26 3/8 in. (71.4 x 67 cm)
Private collection, USA

WAR AND REVOLUTION IN RUSSIA: 1914–1922   JO-ANNE BIRNIE DANZKER

Only one month after the Carnegie's Annual Exhibition closed in Pittsburgh, on July 28, 1914, the Austro-Hungarian Empire declared war on Serbia, and World War I began. Communications between Russia and the United States became very difficult, and contact with Fechin ceased.[44] As collector John R. Hunter would later recall, there was a long silence until around 1919, when a letter arrived from Nicolai Fechin recounting the hardships and famine he and his young family had experienced during the war and the Russian Revolution.[45] Both Hunter and fellow collector William S. Stimmel began seeking a way to bring Fechin to the United States. It was not until June 1922, however, that a letter was received from the district supervisor of the American Relief Administration in Kazan stating that Fechin was anxious to leave Russia.[46] While Hunter pursued avenues at the highest levels of government, Fechin sold canvases to a member of the American Relief Administration in Kazan and to Stimmel[47] in order to raise $700 with which to travel by ship from Riga, Latvia, to New York. With the support of Stephen G. Porter, chairman of the U.S. Committee of Foreign Affairs, who declared Fechin's petition to enter the United States a "most meritorious and urgent case," Fechin finally received approval and he and his family arrived in the United States in August 1923.[48]

Despite their difficulties with contacting Fechin before 1919, Hunter and Stimmel had ensured that he was represented in important exhibitions in the United States by lending paintings from their collections. In 1915, Stimmel lent *Lady in Pink* (p. 11) to the Panama-Pacific International Exposition in San Francisco, where it was exhibited in the International Section together with the work of Pierre Puvis de Chavannes, Claude Monet, Camille Pissarro, Pierre-Auguste Renoir, and Alfred Sisley.[49] Eugen Neuhaus described seeing *Lady in Pink* in this setting:

> On the west wall opposite the Puvis [de Chavannes] four very different canvases deserve to be mentioned. In the center a young Russian, Nicholas Fechin, displays a very unusual virtuosity in a picture of a somewhat sensual-looking young creature. Aside from the fascination of this young human animal, the handling of paint in this canvas is most extraordinary, possessing a technical quality few other canvases in the entire exhibition have. There is life, such as very few painters ever attain, and seen only in the work of a master. . . . I have a strange fondness for this weird canvas.[50]

Following Fechin's successful American debut at the Carnegie Institute's Annual Exhibition in Pittsburgh in 1910, his paintings were eagerly sought by American collectors, in particular William S. Stimmel of Pittsburgh and George A. Hearn of New York, who each purchased a painting from the exhibition. Given the limited number of Fechin's canvases available for purchase through exhibitions in the United States, Stimmel and his business associate, John R. Hunter of Pittsburgh, began acquiring paintings directly from Fechin in Russia based on photographs he would send. Hunter's first such purchase was *Nude Figure*, 1911, followed by five additional acquisitions including *Portrait of a Young Woman*, 1912 (p. 31). As a result of these purchases, important paintings associated with Fechin's Russian period (1909-23) were to be found in the United States rather than in Russia in the early twentieth century.

Nude Figure, 1911
Oil on canvas
28 1/2 x 26 in. (72.39 x 66.04 cm)
The Filatov Family Art Foundation

Portrait of Miss Kitaeva, 1912
Oil on canvas
35 1/2 x 30 in. (90.17 x 76.2 cm)
The Dr. and Mrs. Charles R. Briggs Collection

Portrait of a Young Woman, 1912
Oil on canvas
31 3/4 x 28 in. (80.65 x 71.12 cm)
Frye Art Museum, 1990.006

One of the members of the International Jury of the 1915 Panama-Pacific International Exposition in San Francisco was Christian Brinton, who had admired Fechin's *Portrait of Kissa* three years earlier at the Carnegie.[51] Brinton published his impressions of the Panama-Pacific International and San Diego Expositions and chose to illustrate his essay, "The Modern Spirit in Contemporary Painting," with a reproduction of *Lady in Pink* (p. 11).[52] Although he did not refer specifically to Fechin, Brinton made an observation about the "new art" of the day that certainly applied to Fechin's "disorderly" artistic practice: "Social as well as aesthetic in aspect, it bases itself upon an unfettered, uncompromising individualism."[53]

In November 1919, Brinton gave the inaugural address at the First Annual Exhibition of Contemporary International Art in Dallas; among the artists represented was Nicolai Fechin, with *Lady in Pink* and *Portrait of a Russian Actress*, both on loan from Stimmel.[54] With the reinstatement of the Annual Exhibition at the Carnegie Institute in the spring of 1920, Fechin was again present with *Portrait of Abramotchiff* (Portrait of Abramichev). Although the exhibition catalogue does not state that this painting was on loan,[55] it was likely borrowed from the collection of John R. Hunter.[56] With contact reestablished between Fechin and his collectors in Pittsburgh in 1922 through the diplomat and American Relief Administration worker J. Rives Childs,[57] the difficult years of deprivation and loss for Fechin's family drew to a close. The American years were about to begin.

NEW YORK: 1923–1927   JO-ANNE BIRNIE DANZKER

Nicolai Fechin and his family first saw "the fantastic skyline of New York" through a thick fog on August 1, 1923.[58] His loyal supporters John R. Hunter and William S. Stimmel arranged for Fechin to be greeted by the Lithuanian émigré painter Aaron Harry Gorson (1872–1933), who helped the new arrivals find accommodations.[59] Stimmel introduced Fechin to several gallerists. Although he apparently did not bring paintings with him, Fechin showed Hunter charcoal drawings from Russia, which the collector greatly admired. In the first days after his arrival, Fechin painted *Eya with Cantaloupe*, 1923 (p. 61), and Hunter purchased it before it was finished.[60] Around this time, Fechin also completed three portraits of his wife that are notable for their disparate styles and painterly techniques: *Alexandra Fechin,* ca. 1923–33 (p. 39), *Lady in Black (Portrait of Alexandra Belkovich Fechin)*, 1924 (p. 40), and *Portrait of the Artist's Wife*, 1925 (p. 41).

In these first heady months in the United States, an important solo exhibition of Fechin's work at the Art Institute of Chicago was organized at the initiative of its director, Robert B. Harshe, the former associate director of the Fine Arts Department at the Carnegie Institute. Harshe asked collectors Stimmel, Hunter, Clarkson Cowl, Edward Duff Balken, and J. Rives Childs—who had assisted Fechin in leaving Russia—to lend paintings for the exhibition that opened on December 20, 1923.[61] Among the paintings on display were *Portrait of Miss Sapojnikoff*, 1908 (p. 13), *Portrait* (study) (*Portrait of Nina Belkovich*), 1910 (p. 22), *Nude Figure*, 1911 (p. 29), *Lady in Pink*, 1912 (p. 11), *Portrait of a Young Woman*, 1912 (p. 31), and *The Artist Burliuk*, 1923 (p. 35). The Ukrainian artist David Burliuk (1882–1967) had first met Fechin when he studied in Kazan before moving to the Royal Academy of Arts in Munich in 1902. Here, he made contact with Wassily Kandinsky and was invited to participate in the influential *Blue Rider* exhibition in 1911. Burliuk, commonly known as the father of Russian Futurism, had moved to New York in 1922 and met Fechin by chance.[62]

Before Fechin's arrival in New York, both he and Burliuk were included in the landmark *Exhibition of Russian Painting and Sculpture* at the Brooklyn Art Museum from February 24 to April 6, 1923.[63] Among the 277 paintings and forty-eight sculptures in the exhibition by artists such as Alexander Archipenko, Léon Bakst, Natalia Goncharova, Wassily Kandinsky, and Mikhail Larionov were thirty-one paintings from Burliuk and eighteen canvases by Fechin, among which *Portrait of Miss Sapojnikoff* (p. 13) and *Lady in Pink* (p. 11) were illustrated. Two portraits of Fechin's father were also included as well as *Portrait of a Young Woman* (p. 31) and *Nude Figure* (p. 29).[64] In his introductory essay, Christian Brinton describes Fechin as a representative of Russian realism:

Nikolai Evreinov (1879–1953) was a renowned Russian playwright and director who experimented with "reconstructing the spectator" in *The Storming of the Winter Palace* (1920), a mass spectacle staged in the aftermath of the Revolution, in which around a thousand spectators and performers took part.[h] A fierce critic of the naturalism favored by Konstantin Stanislavski at the Moscow Art Theatre, Evreinov wrote the experimental monodrama *The Theatre of the Soul* (1911), which reputedly inspired Man Ray to create his aerograph *Suicide* (originally *The Theatre of the Soul*) in 1917. Man Ray later published the monodrama in English.[i] Today, Evreinov is best known for *A Merry Death* (1909) and *The Main Thing* (1921), which was presented in New York in 1926 under the title *The Chief Thing*, with Edward G. Robinson in the role of the Stage Director. Fechin may have painted *Portrait of a Writer (Nikolai N. Evreinov)* on the occasion of the play's Broadway premiere at the Guild Theater, today the August Wilson Theatre.

Portrait of a Writer (Nikolai N. Evreinov), 1926
Oil on canvas
30 x 25 in. (76.2 x 63.5 cm)
Frye Art Museum, 1991.006

Shortly after Fechin's arrival in New York in 1923, a solo exhibition of his work opened at the Art Institute of Chicago on the initiative of its director, Robert B. Harshe. Among the paintings on display was *Portrait of the Russian Painter, David Burliuk*. Fechin first met Burliuk (1882–1967) when they were studying in Kazan. In 1902, Burliuk moved to the Royal Academy of Arts in Munich, where he met Wassily Kandinsky, who invited him to participate in the *Blue Rider* exhibition of 1911. Burliuk, commonly known as the father of Russian Futurism, moved in 1922 to New York, where he met Fechin by chance a year later. Both Fechin and Burliuk were included in the *Exhibition of Russian Painting and Sculpture* at the Brooklyn Museum in 1923. Among the 277 paintings and 48 sculptures in the exhibition by artists such as Alexander Archipenko, Léon Bakst, Natalia Goncharova, Wassily Kandinsky, and Mikhail Larionov were 31 paintings by Burliuk and 18 canvases by Fechin. According to newspaper reports, Fechin's portrait of Burliuk was possibly included in the Carnegie Institute's International Exhibition in 1925.[1]

The Artist Burliuk, 1923
Oil on canvas
49 1/8 x 33 1/4 in. (124.8 x 84.5 cm)
Collection of the New Mexico Museum of Art,
Gift of Edwin C. Lineberry in Memory of Duane
Van Vechten Lineberry, 1980 (4607.23P)

Eya, ca. 1923–26
Oil on canvas
16 5/8 x 12 5/8 in. (42.2 x 32.2 cm)
Stark Museum of Art,
Orange, Texas, 31.28.36

> The foremost exponent of Russian realism is the masterful Cossack, Ilya Repin, and in a measure the mantle of Repin has descended upon the shoulders of one of his favourite pupils, Nikolai Fechin. In its essential features the art of Fechin is Repinesque. You note in these portraits and character studies from the picturesque, semi-Tatar district about Kazan, provincial types in all their primitive verity. Fechin . . . returned [to Kazan] after his 'prentice days at the Imperial Academy to depict that life and scene for which he evinces such abiding sympathy.[65]

Several months later, Stimmel and Hunter commissioned Brinton to write the essay for the catalogue of Fechin's solo exhibition at the Art Institute of Chicago.[66] Here again, he proposed that Fechin's art "bases itself upon observation and simple verity of vision and rendering"[67] and "upon discriminating analysis of the simple and actual, and upon sound, disciplined craftsmanship."[68] For Brinton, Fechin belonged "with the frankly objective protagonists of Russian painting," his canvases revealing a "permeating pessimism" and "the sober, searching veritism of the Moscow Art Theater."[69] Brinton's insistence on perceiving Fechin as pursuing the frankly objective is, however, at odds with the complexity of the artist's canvases, which both reflect and deny an impulse to verism. Indeed, in 1926, Fechin would paint *Portrait of a Writer (Nikolai N. Evreinov)* (p. 34), a depiction of one of the fiercest critics of realism and the Moscow Art Theatre of Konstantin Stanislavski. It is possible that the portrait was made on the occasion of the Broadway premiere of Evreinov's *The Chief Thing*, with Edward G. Robinson, at the Guild Theatre.[70]

In New York, Fechin was also welcomed at the new Grand Central School of Art founded by artists Edmund William Greacen, Walter Leighton Clark, and John Singer Sargent, who offered him a teaching position. The school, situated in the east wing of New York's Grand Central Terminal, was run by an artists' cooperative, the Grand Central Art Galleries. Among his students, and later his teaching colleague, was the Armenian artist Arshile Gorky (1904?–1948), an admirer of Fechin's techniques. Photographer Stergis M. Stergis claimed of a work by Gorky that he owned, "You'd think it was painted by Fechin."[71] Success continued with recognition at the National Academy of Design in New York in 1924 and at the 1926 Sesquicentennial International Exposition in Philadelphia, and at an exhibition at the Saint Louis Art Museum in March 1926.[72] The excitement of Fechin's new life would draw to a close in 1927, when he became ill and was forced to leave New York for his health.

Nude with Shell, ca. 1923–1926
Oil on canvas
24 1/8 x 20 in. (61.3 x 50.8 cm)
Private collection, USA

Alexandra Fechin, ca. 1923–1933
Oil on stretched canvas
24 x 20 in. (60.96 x 50.8 cm)
Panhandle-Plains Historical Museum,
Canyon, Texas, Johnie Griffin
Collection, 1501/58

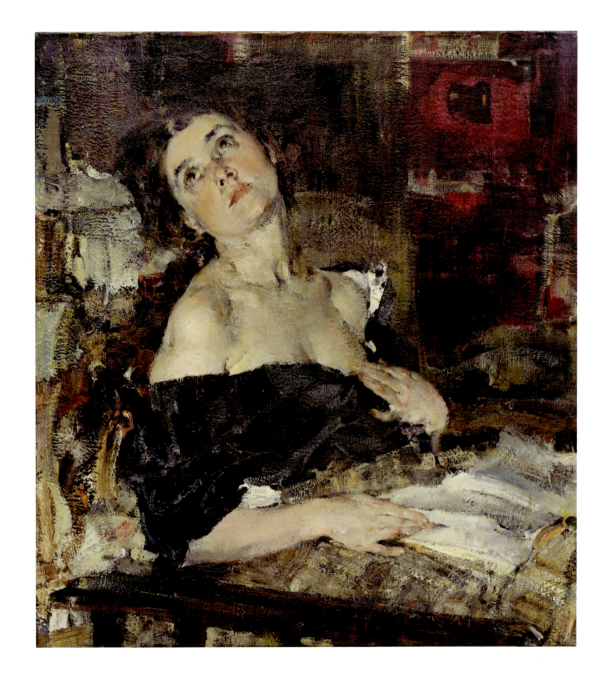

By all accounts, Nicolai Fechin was deeply attached to his wife, Alexandra. Independent, capable, and strong-willed, she sustained the family during the difficult years of the Russian Revolution, maintaining their home in the village of Vasilievo while Fechin remained in Kazan and taught at the School of Art. When they arrived in the United States in September 1923, Alexandra played an important role in helping her family adjust to their new life. Their friend, the writer Frank Waters, later remembered, "When they first arrived in New York, [Alexandra] had learned English much more quickly than Fechin and was a great help to him while he painted portraits. He never said a word, depending upon her to instruct the sitter how to pose and make small talk so the subject would not become nervous."[k] In these first years in their new home, Fechin completed three portraits of his wife that are notable for their disparate styles and painterly techniques: *Alexandra Fechin*, ca. 1923–33 (p. 39), *Lady in Black (Portrait of Alexandra Belkovich Fechin)*, 1924, and *Portrait of the Artist's Wife*, 1925 (p. 41).

Lady in Black (Portrait of Alexandra Belkovich Fechin), 1924
Oil on canvas
35 x 32 in. (88.9 x 81.28 cm)
Frye Art Museum, 1982.018

Portrait of the Artist's Wife, 1925
Oil on canvas
36 5/8 x 31 1/8 in. (93 x 79 cm)
The Filatov Family Art Foundation

LAUREN PALMOR   TAOS AND CALIFORNIA: 1927–1955

In the summer of 1926, the Scottish American painter John Young-Hunter (1874–1955), a former student of John Singer Sargent's who kept a studio in Taos, New Mexico,[73] invited Nicolai Fechin and his family to visit the Southwest. During this time, Fechin met the celebrated patron of the arts Mabel Dodge Luhan. In Taos, he found artistic exchange and lively conversations orchestrated by Luhan who was a renowned *salonnière*. The atmosphere of an art colony and the New Mexico landscape inspired writers and artists, including Marsden Hartley, D. H. Lawrence, and Georgia O'Keeffe.

Back in New York, Fechin fell ill in the winter of 1927 and moved with his family to Taos, where the air was believed to possess healing qualities. He painted portraits of the cultural elite, much as he had done in New York and, earlier, in Russia. One such subject was the radio personality and political radical Muriel Draper (p. 43), who visited Luhan in New Mexico in 1933. Fechin also portrayed the indigenous peoples of the region. He was attracted by their rich culture and ancient traditions. These portraits, distinguished by their bold colors and bravura technique, form a distinctive chapter within his oeuvre. Pictures such as *Joe with Drum*, ca. 1927–1933 (p. 51), the charcoal drawing *Indian Profile*, ca. 1927–1933 (p. 49), and *Albidia*, 1928 (p. 53), a portrait of Albidia Marcus Reyna (1896–1960), Luhan's maid and housekeeper, exemplify his depictions of his adopted community.

Luhan once described Taos as "the dawn of the world,"[74] and for Fechin, the move marked a new beginning. By most accounts, Taos was an ideal environment for painting. The small village deep in the Sangre de Cristo Mountains was a place where one could find aspen groves, cottonwood trees, and piñon pine forests.[75] Fechin's interest in landscape revived, and he painted the changing seasons in New Mexico, as seen in *Winter Landscape, Taos*, ca. 1927–1933 (p. 62). The *Los Angeles Times* noted in 1928 that Fechin had also traveled

Portrait of a Man (possibly William Randolph Hearst), n.d.
Charcoal on laid paper
17 1/2 x 14 in. (44.45 x 35.56 cm)
Frye Art Museum, 1981.001

Muriel Draper, n.d. (ca. 1933)
Charcoal on paper
16 7/8 x 13 in. (42.86 x 33.02 cm)
Frye Art Museum, 1986.008

to Southern California, where he applied "his unusual gifts as a luminist" in depicting the landscape, "finding sympathetic material in the burnt summer hills and the shimmer of sunlight on cactus and yucca."[76] Examples of Fechin's Californian landscapes include *Andreas Canyon*, n.d. (p. 65), and *La Jolla Landscape*, n.d. (p. 64).

This period of bold colors, experimentation, and enchantment with New Mexico and its people was to be short-lived. Alexandra Belkovich Fechin asked her husband for a divorce in 1933. Their daughter, portrayed the same year in *Eya in Peasant Blouse* (p. 60), would remain with her father. Fechin returned briefly to New York in the winter of 1933 before settling in the Los Angeles area, thus concluding a significant period in his life.

In 1936, Fechin traveled to Mexico with a small group of artists, visiting Guadalajara, Mexico City, and Oaxaca. Among the group was his student Katherine Benepe Shackelford, who later recalled that "we generally painted in my room because it had the best light. . . . The sources of supply for materials were fair only; in the south, nothing. . . . Artists in the area found other supplies for us."[77] According to a newspaper report, Fechin spent three months in Mexico in 1938, a journey that yielded *Juan the Peon* (p. 67), which Fechin exhibited in Los Angeles the following year.[78] In 1938, Fechin visited Japan, Java, and Bali with Milan Rupert, a collector and scholar of oriental art. In Bali, Fechin established a studio in Denpasar and produced drawings such as *Balinese Girl with Earrings*, 1938 (p. 68), and paintings such as *Temple Dancer*, 1938 (p. 69).

Following his sojourn in Bali, Fechin traveled little and spent his last years in Santa Monica, California, where he taught Saturday painting classes in his home studio. He passed away in his sleep on October 5, 1955.

Profile of a Woman, n.d.
Charcoal on laid paper
18 1/8 x 13 3/8 in. (46.04 x 33.97 cm)
Frye Art Museum, 1982.012

Young Girl, California, n.d.
Charcoal on laid paper
16 7/8 x 13 3/4 in. (42.86 x 34.92 cm)
Frye Art Museum, 1977.007

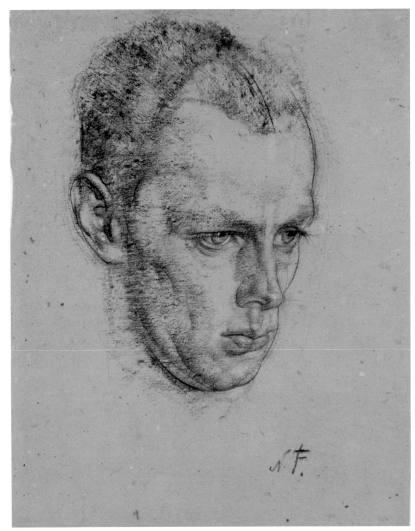

Young Woman, n.d.
Charcoal on paper
18 1/4 x 14 1/4 in. (46.36 x 36.2 cm)
Frye Art Museum, 1979.017

Young Man, n.d.
Charcoal on laid paper
18 1/8 x 13 1/2 in. (46.04 x 34.29 cm)
Frye Art Museum, 1979.016

Reclining Nude, n.d.
Charcoal on laid paper
12 5/8 x 17 in. (32.07 x 43.18 cm)
Frye Art Museum, 1986.009

Seated Male Nude, n.d.
Charcoal on laid paper
17 1/8 x 12 3/8 in. (43.5 x 31.43 cm)
Frye Art Museum, 1976.008

Nude Study, 1920
Charcoal on paper
23 1/4 x 16 1/4 in. (59.05 x 41.27 cm)
Courtesy of Gerald Peters Gallery

Indian Profile, ca. 1927–1933
Charcoal on paper
17 1/2 x 13 in. (44.37 x 33 cm)
Private collection, USA

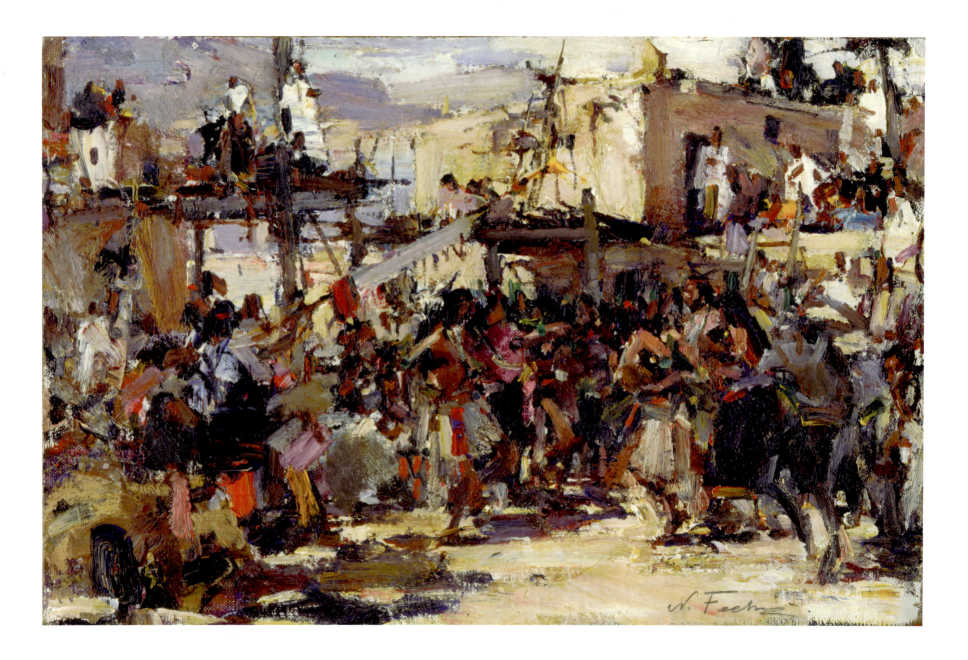

The Indian Dancers, ca. 1945
Oil on canvas on panel
12 3/4 x 19 1/2 in. (32.4 x 49.5 cm)
Stark Museum of Art, Orange,
Texas, 31.28.46

Joe with Drum, ca. 1927–1933
Oil on canvas
24 x 20 in. (61 x 50.8 cm)
Stark Museum of Art, Orange,
Texas, 31.28.39

This painting depicts Albidia Marcus Reyna, maid and housekeeper for Mabel Dodge Luhan (1879–1962), a philanthropist and celebrated patron of the arts who moved to Taos, New Mexico, in 1919. Among the influential writers and artists hosted by Luhan were D. H. Lawrence, Willa Cather, Ansel Adams, Marsden Hartley, and Georgia O'Keeffe. Albidia was a popular model who sat for a number of artists in Taos, including Fechin. In a tribute to Albidia published in *The Horse Fly* on December 22, 1960, John Evans wrote, "She was as beautiful in spirit as she was in body. She possessed that indefinable air of mystery and allure with which only women of true inner beauty can ever really be endowed."[l] Luhan described Albidia as being "like a Persian miniature with her black hair and long, dark eyes."[m]

Albidia, 1928
Oil on canvas
30 1/4 x 25 1/4 in. (76.84 x 64.14 cm)
Frye Art Museum, 1976.003

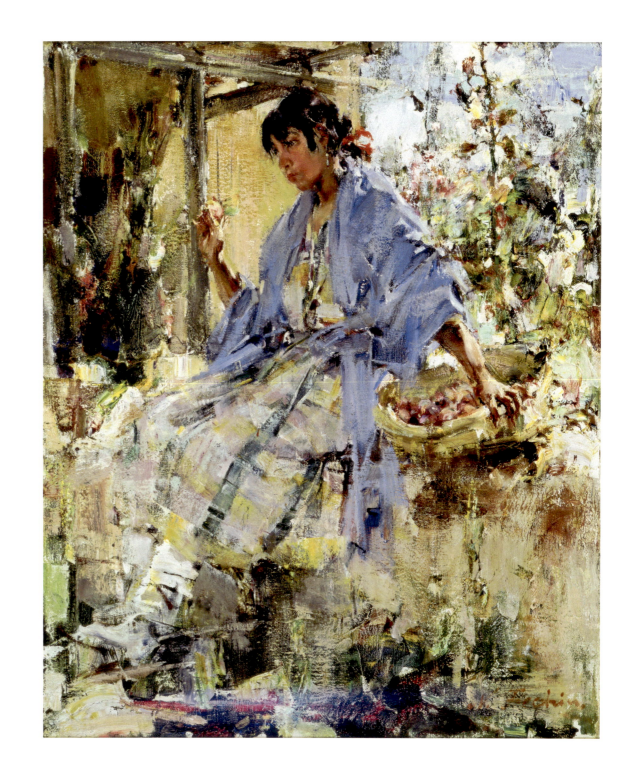

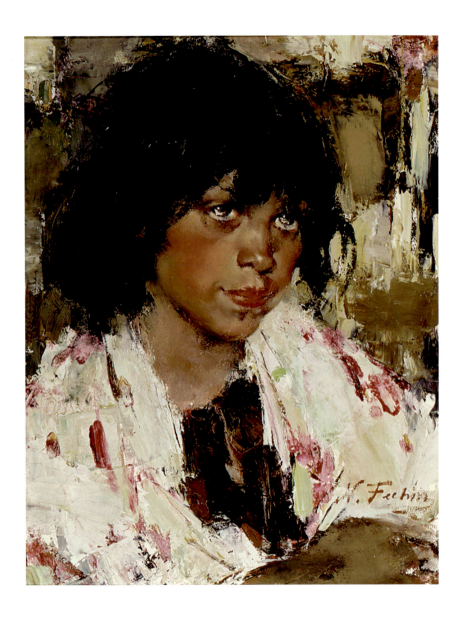

Taosita, ca. 1930
Oil on linen
20 1/4 x 15 1/4 in. (51.44 x 38.74 cm)
Frye Art Museum, 1992.008

In 1912, painter and critic Arthur Hoeber described Fechin's skill in depicting the humble life of the Russian peasant. "It would be a joy," he added, "to see Fechin have a try at American life and conditions with his enormous facility and talent."[n] More than twenty years later, Fechin would portray the life of Native Americans in Taos. In February 1930, the *Los Angeles Times* published an illustration of *Taosita*, under the title *Nana of Taos*, to accompany the announcement of an exhibition of Fechin's paintings at the Stendahl Galleries in the Ambassador Hotel in Los Angeles. In an adjacent photograph, Fechin is shown at work on the painting *Taos Indian Girl*; resting on the floor, against the wall, is *Taosita*.[o] Two weeks later, in a review of the exhibition in the *Los Angeles Times*, Fred Hogue noted that every inch of Fechin's new paintings radiated light and color: "He uses paint extravagantly, layer after layer on the canvas." Hogue also observed, "Either Fechin lapses occasionally into Tartar types in painting the Indians of New Mexico, or the resemblance between the two is closer than I have known."[p]

Friends, n.d.
Oil on canvas
30 1/4 x 19 1/4 in. (76.71 x 48.77 cm)
The Filatov Family Art Foundation

Still Life with Teapot No. 2, ca. 1950s
Oil on canvas
24 x 20 in. (61 x 51 cm)
The Sepherot Foundation Collection,
Liechtenstein

Still Life with Oranges, 1925
Oil on canvas
30 1/4 x 36 1/4 in. (76.835 x 92.075 cm)
Frye Art Museum, 1984.003

Daisies, 1930
Oil on canvas
24 x 20 in. (60.96 x 50.8 cm)
The Filatov Family Art Foundation

The Samovar, n.d.
Oil on canvas
25 3/4 x 33 3/4 in. (65.4 x 85.72 cm)
Frye Art Museum, 1989.002

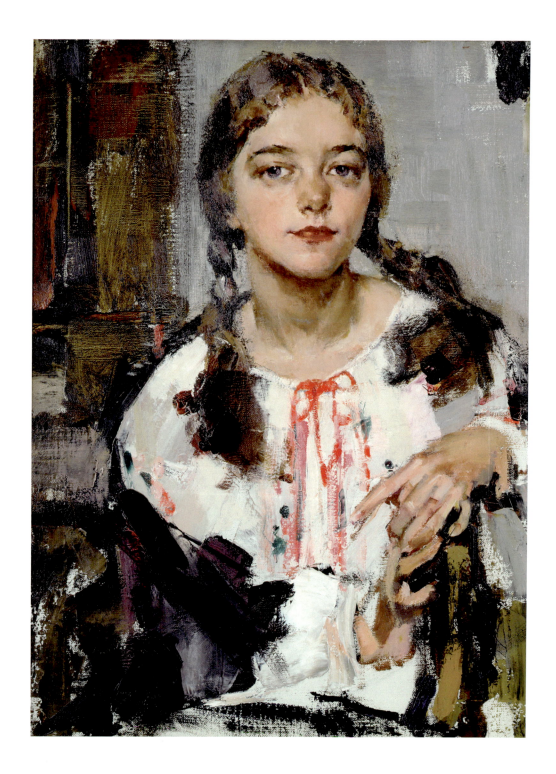

In the first days after his arrival in New York in September 1923, Fechin began *Eya with Cantaloupe*, a portrait of his nine-year-old daughter. John R. Hunter, who, with William S. Stimmel, had been instrumental in bringing Fechin and his family to the United States, recalled in 1959, "Even before I arrived in New York, he ... was working on a canvas 32 x 34 in., a portrait of his daughter, Eya, sitting beside a table with a large assortment of fruit. I purchased that painting before it was finished." Hunter added, "It still hangs in the living room of my apartment and is much admired by my friends."[q]

Eya in Peasant Blouse was completed in 1933, the year in which Alexandra asked her husband for a divorce. Eya is nineteen here, the same age as Alexandra when Fechin portrayed her in 1911 (p. 23). In 1975, Eya Fechin Branham recalled, "Posing for him as a child developed in me an unusual physical control which eventually made me study dance and later practice dance therapy."[r]

Eya in Peasant Blouse, 1933
Oil on canvas
24 x 19 7/8 in. (61 x 50.3 cm)
Private collection, USA

Eya with Cantaloupe, 1923
Oil on canvas
32 1/2 x 34 1/2 in. (82.6 x 87.6 cm)
Private collection, ID

Winter Landscape, Taos, ca. 1927–1933
Oil on canvas
15 1/4 x 24 1/4 in. (38.7 x 61.6 cm)
Private Collection of Tia

Beaver Dam, 1930
Oil on canvas
25 x 30 in. (63.5 x 76.2 cm)
The Filatov Family Art Foundation

La Jolla Landscape, n.d.
Oil on canvas
24 1/4 x 30 1/4 in. (61.6 x 76.84 cm)
Frye Art Museum, 1975.013

Andreas Canyon, n.d.
Oil on canvas
24 1/8 x 32 1/8 in. (61.28 x 81.6 cm)
Frye Art Museum, 1977.017

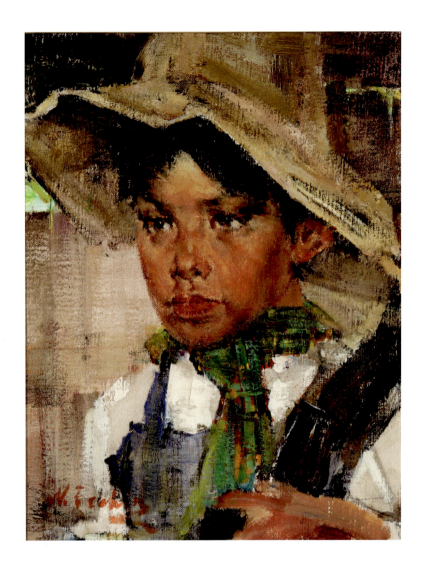

According to Katherine Benepe Shackelford (1899–1988), a student of Fechin's, she and a small group of artists traveled to Mexico with Fechin in 1936. During the tour, which included Guadalajara, Mexico City, and Oaxaca, Fechin took photographs and made drawings. Fred Hogue suggested in the *Los Angeles Times* that Fechin had spent three months in Mexico in 1938 and that *Juan the Peon* might have been the only completed painting brought back from this journey.[5] This painting reflects Fechin's lifelong pleasure in conflating unadorned sociological portraits and virtuoso displays of paint and color.

Mexican Boy, ca. 1945–1947
Oil on canvas
18 x 14 in. (45.72 x 35.56 cm)
Private Collection of Tia

Juan the Peon, 1938
Oil on linen
24 x 20 1/8 in. (60.96 x 51.12 cm)
Frye Art Museum, 1986.006

Fechin enjoyed his last period of extensive travel in 1938, when he visited the Indonesian island of Bali with his friend Milan Rupert, a collector and dealer of Oriental art. Although the pair had originally intended to travel widely across Asia, they stayed in Bali for five months, and Fechin established a studio in Denpasar. Rupert, who spoke Malay, brought models to the studio. Fechin traveled around the island with his camera and photographed extensively in the surrounding kampongs. Fechin's portraits from Bali reflect his lifelong interest in indigenous and traditional cultures.

Balinese Girl with Earrings, 1938
Charcoal on laid paper
16 3/4 x 13 3/4 in. (42.54 x 34.92 cm)
Frye Art Museum, 1980.006

Temple Dancer, 1938
Oil on canvas
17 3/4 x 14 3/4 in. (45 x 37.5 cm)
Courtesy of Kournikova Gallery, Moscow

Self-Portrait, after 1948
Oil on canvas
23 5/8 x 19 7/8 in. (60 x 50.3 cm)
Private collection, Russia

BIOGRAPHY

Nicolai Ivanovich Fechin (1881–1955) was born in Kazan, the capital of the Republic of Tatarstan on the Volga River. His father was a craftsman who carved icons and altars for the Russian Orthodox Church, and Fechin assisted his father in the workshop until he entered the Kazan School of Art shortly after its founding in 1895. After graduating from the school in 1901, he passed the entrance examination for the Imperial Academy of Arts in Saint Petersburg, where he would study under Ilya Repin (1844–1930), the noted Russian painter.

Upon graduating from the academy in 1909, Fechin received a scholarship that enabled him to tour western Europe before he returned to Kazan to take up a teaching post at the School of Art. The same year, the Imperial Academy of Arts submitted one of the paintings he had completed in his graduating year to an international exhibition in Munich, where it was awarded a medal. In 1910, Fechin was invited to exhibit at the Annual Exhibition at the Carnegie Institute in Pittsburgh, Pennsylvania. His paintings, *Portrait of Mlle. Lapojnikoff* [Sapojnikoff] and *Portrait of My Father*, caught the attention of New York patron of the arts George A. Hearn and Pittsburgh collector William S. Stimmel, who both began purchasing Fechin's paintings on a regular basis. In addition to participating regularly in the Annual Exhibitions at the Carnegie Institute (1910–14, 1920), Fechin was also represented at the joint International Exhibition of the Munich Secession and Munich Künstlergenossenschaft (Artists' Association) in 1909 and 1913, the International Exhibition of the Munich Secession (1910), the Winter Exhibition of the National Academy of Design in New York (1911), the International Exposition of Rome (1911), the Venice Biennale (1914), the Panama-Pacific International Exposition in San Francisco (1915), and the First Annual Exhibition of Contemporary International Art in Dallas (1919).

In 1913, Fechin married Alexandra Belkovich, the daughter of one of the founders of the Kazan School of Art, and their daughter, Eya, was born a year later. With the outbreak of war in Europe in 1914 and the Russian Revolution in 1917, living conditions in Kazan became very difficult. Alexandra and Eya moved to the village of Vasilievo, twenty miles outside of Kazan, while Fechin remained in the city and taught at the School of Art. Famine and disease reached Kazan, and in 1919, both of Fechin's parents succumbed to typhoid within months of each other. With the support of Stimmel and fellow American collector John R. Hunter, Fechin and his family were allowed to emigrate to the United States and arrived in New York by steamship on August 1, 1923.

Fechin's American career began in New York with a teaching post at the Grand Central School of Art, cofounded by John Singer Sargent. Here he met Arshile Gorky (1904?–1948), who greatly admired his work. Fechin enjoyed success as an artist, participating in a major presentation of Russian art organized by the Brooklyn Museum and in a solo exhibition of his paintings at the Art Institute of Chicago in 1923. The following year, he exhibited again at the National Academy of Design, and in 1926, he participated in the Sesquicentennial International Exposition in Philadelphia and had a solo exhibition at the Saint Louis Art Museum. That same year, the Fechin family received an invitation to visit Taos, New Mexico.

In 1927, Fechin became ill and decided to move with his family to Taos, which offered good air and the support of a vital art community. In Taos he built his own home as a *Gesamtkunstwerk*, or total work of art, and began painting portraits of the indigenous peoples of the region.

Following the dissolution of his marriage in 1933, Fechin and his daughter Eya returned to New York before moving to Los Angeles. With the exception of journeys to Mexico and a visit to Bali, Fechin remained in Southern California for the last two decades of his life, teaching and painting until his death in 1955.

The Lace Collar, n.d.
Oil and tempera on canvas
30 x 25 in. (76.2 x 63.5 cm)
Private collection, Russia

Although this painting is known as *The Lace Collar*, a partially visible label attached to the verso of the frame states that the picture is a portrait of "Mrs. L. (?) Montgomery." It is possible that the sitter is Lorena Montgomery née Lloyd (1867–1959), who, with her husband, Melville Montgomery, was an important patron and supporter of Fechin's in the last years of his life. Confined following a car accident, Lorena Montgomery began to draw and asked Fechin if she could study under him. In May 1941, the Stendahl Galleries in Los Angeles presented thirty-seven of her paintings together with the sculpture of her sister-in-law Caroline A. Lloyd (1875–1945).¹

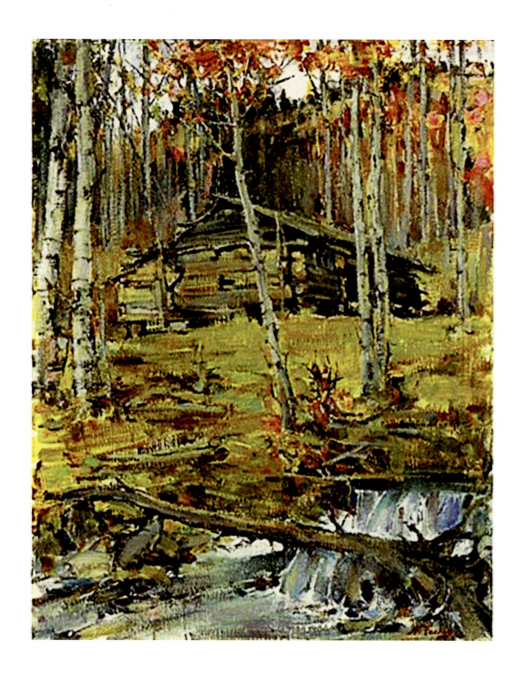

Autumn Trees, Twining, n.d.
Oil on canvas
30 x 24 in. (76.2 by 61 cm)
The Gil Waldman Collection

NOTES

FOREWORD

1. *The Craftsman* 21, no. 5 (February 1912): 489.

INTERNATIONAL SUCCESS: 1909–1914

1. Fechin's canvas, *Bearing Off the Bride*, was described as follows:
"The savage splendid heterogeneous canvas of Nicholas Fechin which has place of honor in the Vanderbilt Gallery and the ultra-modern, distinguished aesthetic portrait of William Chase, which hangs near it at the right . . . a distinctive style, too, which stands out from Fechin's barbaric mastery of form and color all the more convincingly because of contrast. It would be hard to realize how essentially modern and American Chase is without Fechin close at the left, and still harder to realize how wholly savage and remote from what we call civilization, yet how magnificent in its presentation of native traditions the best of Russian art is, without seeing Fechin in the Vanderbilt Gallery."
The Craftsman 21, no. 5 (February 1912): 489.

2. *Illustrated Catalogue, National Academy of Design Winter Exhibition 1911* (New York: National Academy of Design, 1911), 36, cat. 308. The exhibition took place from December 9, 1911, to January 7, 1912. See also "Fechin's Clever Canvas," *American Art News* 10, no. 12 (December 30, 1911): 1.

3. The Mari live primarily in the Mari El and the Tatarstan and Bashkortostan Republics. According to Galina P. Tuluzakova, the painting was inspired by Fechin's travels to remote villages outside Kazan during the summers of 1906 and 1907 and depicts a wedding ritual performed in the village of Lipsha.

4. See "George A. Hearn Dies of Pleurisy; Prominent Merchant and Art Collector Gave Much to Metropolitan Museum," *New York Times*, December 2, 1913, http://query.nytimes.com/gst/abstract.htm l?res=F20817FB3B5B13738DDDAB0894DA415B838DF1D3 (accessed December 2012). Fechin's *Bearing Off the Bride* was sold to Hearn's son-in-law George B. Wheeler for $1,500 and *Portrait of Miss Lapojnikoff* [Sapojnikoff] to W. S. Stimmel of Pittsburgh for $1,325 at the auction of the Hearn Collection on February 27, 1918. At the same auction, a painting by Courbet sold for $1,250, and one by Constable for $650. *American Art News* 16, no. 21 (March 2, 1918).

5. "Fechin's Clever Canvas," *American Art News* 10, no. 12 (December 30, 1911): 1.

6. F.J.M. Jr., "Art: The Winter Academy," *Nation* 93, no. 2426 (December 28, 1911): 638, http://books.google.com/books?id=w_oxAQAAIAAJ&pg=PA638&lpg=PA638&dq=Fechin+carrying+off+the+bride&source=bl&ots=vpY-5Ki6X9&sig=YNLO1jmeRvV3J1IOoCkhpshzz4Q&hl=en&sa=X &ei=OpT fUKqENcqXiALc_YHIDA&sqi=2&ved=0CDoQ6AEwAg#v=onepage&q=Fechin%20carrying%20off%20the%20bride&f=false (accessed December 2012).

7. In *American Art News* 10, no. 9 (December 9, 1911): 7, the following was noted:
"There are a number of exceedingly good pictures; but none that can be called 'star' canvases, save the large composition, 'Bearing Off the Bride,' by Nicholas Fechin, the Russian, shown at the last Carnegie Institute display, now owned and loaned by Mr. George A. Hearn, which occupies the place of honor, namely, the centre of the North wall of the Vanderbilt Gallery. This canvas, a remarkable work in the cleverness of its technique, character, expression, and story-telling quality, was fully described and praised in the review of the Carnegie Exhibition, published May 7 last. It is a pleasure to know such a remarkably strong picture has come into the possession of so appreciative and generous an art patron as Mr. Hearn, and that it will remain in the country."

8. For *Portrait of Mlle. Lapojnikoff* [Sapojnikoff], cat. no. 81 (illustrated), and *Portrait of My Father*, cat. no. 82, see *Fourteenth Annual Exhibition at the Carnegie Institute* (Pittsburgh, PA: Carnegie Art Galleries, 1910), 11, 80, 81, 241. As there is no illustration of Fechin's portrait of his father, it is uncertain which version was exhibited. The exhibition ran from May 2 to June 13, 1910.

9. "The Carnegie Institute's Exhibition," *Art and Progress* 1, no. 8 (June 1910): 232.

10. "International Exhibition at Pittsburgh," *American Art News* 8, no. 30 (May 7, 1910): 3.

11. *Offizieller Katalog der X. Internationalen Kunstausstellung im kgl. Glaspalast zu München* (Munich: Publisher of the Central Committee of the Tenth International Art Exhibition, 1909), xxi. The Medal, 2nd Class, no. 36, was awarded to "Nicolaus Feschin." The Medal, 1st Class, for Painting was awarded to twenty-five artists, among them Mikhail Vasilyevich Nesterov (1862–1942) from Kiev, who was also associated with the Peredvizhniki, or Itinerants; Max Slevogt from Berlin; and Otto Strützl from Munich. One hundred and three artists were awarded Medals, 2nd Class. Members of the jury representing the Munich Secession included Hugo von Habermann, Albert von Keller, Franz von Stuck, and Fritz von Uhde. The commissioner for Russia was the curator of the Imperial Academy of Fine Arts in Saint Petersburg, Emil von Wiesel, who was also among the committee that awarded medals. Fechin's award of a Medal, 2nd Class, is confirmed in the second edition of the 1913 catalogue for the International Exhibition of the Munich Secession: *Illustrierter Katalog der XI. Internationalen Kunstausstellung im kgl. Glaspalast zu München* (Munich: Pick & Co., 1913), xxxvi.

12. See *Fourteenth Annual Exhibition at the Carnegie Institute*, exh. cat. (Pittsburgh, PA: Carnegie Art Galleries, 1910), no. 81 and 82, and *Fifteenth Annual Exhibition at the Carnegie Institute*, exh. cat. (Pittsburgh, PA: Carnegie Art Galleries, 1911), no. 83 and 84. Both incorrectly state that Fechin was awarded a gold medal in Munich in 1909.

13. For *Studie* (Study), no. 452, room 70, see *Offizieller Katalog der X. Internationalen Kunstausstellung im kgl. Glaspalast zu München* (Munich: Publisher of the Central Committee of the Tenth International Art Exhibition, 1909), 49. The joint exhibition of the Munich Künstlergenossenschaft and the Munich Secession ran from June 1 to October 31, 1909. Galina Tuluzakova has suggested that the *Study* was a portrait later known as *Lady in Lilac*, 1909, now in the possession of the State Russian Museum, Saint Petersburg.

14. Artists representing Russia exhibited their paintings in rooms 69 and 70 of the Glaspalast.

15. For *Porträtstudie*, no. 18, room 4, and *Die Entführung der Braut*, no. 19 (illustrated), room 11, see *Offizieller*

Katalog der Internationalen Kunstausstellung der Münchener Secession (Munich: F. Bruckmann, 1910), 21, 95. The exhibition ran from May 18 to October 31, 1910.

16. "The Winter Academy can lay no claim to cosmopolitanism—one Fechin doesn't make it so—nor indeed to national eminence; in these things it is easily distanced by Pittsburg [sic], Philadelphia, Washington." "The Winter Academy," *Sun* [New York], December 17, 1911, 8.

17. According to James B. Townsend, *Study* was "a half length sketch portrait of a child, which, while it has all his [Fechin's] skill and adroitness, is too slight to satisfy." Townsend, "Annual Carnegie Institute Exhibition," *American Art News* 9, no. 29 (April 29, 1911): 4.

18. For *Bearing Off the Bride*, no. 83 (illus.), and *Study*, no. 84, see *Fifteenth Annual Exhibition at the Carnegie Institute* (Pittsburgh, PA: Carnegie Art Galleries, 1911). The exhibition ran from April 27 to June 30, 1911.

19. *Studio*, no. 75, see *Padiglione russo all'Esposizione Internazionale del 1911*, Russi in Italia, http://www.russinitalia.it/pubblicazioni/padiglione%20russo%201911.pdf (accessed January 2013).

20. According to the 1920 United States Census, William Smith Stimmel of Pittsburgh was born around 1876 in Johnson, Iowa. He died in 1935. A general agent for the John Hancock Mutual Life Insurance Company, Stimmel was an art patron whose collection was exhibited at the Carnegie Institute in 1918; see *Catalogue of Founder's Day Exhibition, MCMXVIII: The Private Collection of Mr. W. S. Stimmel, Paintings by Modern American and Foreign Painters; April the Twenty-Fifth through June the Twenty-Fifth* (Pittsburgh, PA: Carnegie Institute, Department of Fine Arts, 1918). According to a signed statement written by his associate and fellow collector John R. Hunter on May 26, 1959, Stimmel acquired thirteen of Fechin's paintings up to 1922: *Lady in Pink*; *A Little Peasant Boy*; *A Study*; *Portrait of a Young Girl*; *Portrait of My Father*; *Portrait*; *Christmas Singers*; *Village Scene*; *Village Scene*; *My Daughter, Eya*; *Un Pêcheur*; *Portrait of My Father*; and *Portrait of Miss Sapojnikoff* (at auction from the Estate of George A. Hearn). A copy of the statement dated June 20, 1975, is in the Archives of the Frye Art Museum.

21. See note 4.

22. Based on the 1959 statement by John R. Hunter (see n. 20), it is possible that Stimmel acquired the *Study* exhibited at the Carnegie Institute in 1911.

23. John R. Hunter stated that he acquired *Portrait of a Young Woman*, *Portrait of Abramychev* (Portrait of Abramichev), *Nude Figure*, *Spring in the Steppe*, and *Peasant Girl* between 1911 and 1922. J. R Hunter, statement, May 26, 1959 (copy dated June 20, 1975), Archives of the Frye Art Museum. In the catalogue for Fechin's 1923 solo exhibition at the Art Institute of Chicago, however, Hunter is listed as the lender of only *Peasant Girl*, although both *Nude Figure* and *Portrait of Abramichev* were also exhibited. See *Special Exhibition Paintings by Nikolai Fechin* (Chicago: The Art Institute of Chicago, 1923). The exhibition ran from December 18, 1923, to January 20, 1924.

24. The recent exhibition *Nikolai Fechin*, curated by Galina Tuluzakova on the occasion of the 130th anniversary of his birth, toured to the State Museum of Fine Arts of the Republic of Tatarstan Kazan, the State Russian Museum in Saint Petersburg, and the State Tretyakov Gallery in Moscow in 2011 and 2012, and generated a new appreciation for Fechin on the part of art historians, collectors, and the general public in Russia. As a result, a number of these important canvases have left the United States and are today in Europe, among them, *Bearing Off the Bride*.

25. For *Portrait of Kissa*, see *Sixteenth Annual Exhibition at the Carnegie Institute*, exh. cat. (Pittsburgh, PA: Carnegie Institute, 1912), no. 103 (illus.), 11, 99, 101, 294.

26. L.M., "The Carnegie Institute's Exhibition," *Art and Progress* 3, no. 10 (August 1912): 686.

27. "Annual Carnegie Display," *American Art News* 10, no. 29 (April 27, 1912), 4. In 1911, Townsend expressed his disappointment the previous year with *Bearing Off the Bride*, which he described as "technically good, but confused and muddy in color." James B. Townsend, "Annual Carnegie Institute Exhibition," *American Art News* 9, no. 29 (April 29, 1911): 4.

28. Christian Brinton, "International Arts at Pittsburgh," *International Studio* 46, no. 184 (June 1912): lxxxviii.

29. For *Bildnis, Fräulein Podbelsky*, no. 897, room 61, see *Offizieller Katalog der XI. Internationalen Kunstausstellung im Kgl. Glaspalast zu München 1913, veranstaltet von der "Münchener Künstlergenossenschaft" im Verein mit der "Münchener Secession,"* 2nd ed. (Munich: Pick & Co., 1913), 51, 358. The exhibition ran from June 1 to October 31, 1913.

30. "Fechin's Clever Canvas," *American Art News* 10, no. 12 (December 30, 1911): 1.

31. On these two paintings, *Portrait of Mlle. Kitaeve*, no. 87, and *Lady in Pink*, no. 88 (illus.), see *The Catalogue of the Seventeenth Annual Exhibition at the Carnegie Institute* (Pittsburgh, PA: Carnegie Institute, 1913). On sales from the exhibition, see "Works Sold at Pittsburgh," *American Art News* 11, no. 35 (July 19, 1913): 7. In addition to acquiring Fechin's *Lady in Pink*, Stimmel purchased the following paintings from the Carnegie exhibition: *Cherry Blossoms* by E. W. Redfield; *Portrait, Young Woman* by Olga de Bosnanska; *Autumn near Pittsburgh* by Alexander Roche; and *Silver and Black* by Algernon Talmage. On the response of critics, see L. Merrick, "Inter'l Carnegie Show," *American Art News* 11, no. 28 (April 26, 1913): 1, 4; L. Merrick, "Annual Carnegie Display (Second Notice)," *American Art News* 11, no. 29 (May 3, 1913): 3; Anna Seaton-Schmidt, "The Carnegie Institute's Annual Exhibition," *Art and Progress* 4, no. 8 (June 1913): 989. The exhibition ran from April 24 to June 30, 1913.

32. Both paintings were exhibited in room M of the Carnegie Institute. See *The Catalogue of the Seventeenth Annual Exhibition at the Carnegie Institute* (Pittsburgh, PA: Carnegie Institute, 1913).

33. For Nicolai Fechin's *Venditrice di cavoli*, no. 35, see *XI Esposizione Internazionale d'Arte della Città di Venezia* (Venice: Premiate Officine Grafiche C. Ferrari, 1914), vol. 11: 204, 221, http://babel.hathitrust.org/cgi/pt?id=uc1.b3154245#page/204/mode/1up (accessed December 2012).

34. For *Portrait in Sunlight*, no. 115, and *Portrait*, no. 116, see *The Catalogue of the Eighteenth Annual Exhibition at the Carnegie Institute, April 30 to June 30, 1914* (Pittsburgh, PA: Carnegie Institute, 1914), 100–101.

35. James B. Townsend, "Annual Carnegie Display," *American Art News* 12, no. 30 (May 2, 1914): 2.

36. Bozńanska exhibited *Portrait of a Man*, no. 32. See *The Catalogue of the Eighteenth Annual Exhibition at the Carnegie Institute, April 30 to June 30, 1914* (Pittsburgh, PA: Carnegie Institute, 1914), 50. See also W.W.B., "Artists at Pittsburgh," *American Art News* 12, no. 29 (April 25, 1914): 7. Bozńanska studied in Munich in the 1880s and, after 1898, lived in Paris, where she became a member of the Société Nationale des Beaux-Arts. See http://www.thekf.org/about/gallery/artists/Boznanska/ (accessed December 2012).

37. "Annual Exhibition Carnegie Institute," *Fine Arts Journal* 30, no. 6 (June 1914): 293.

38. John Ellis Bowlt, "Through the Glass Darkly: Images of Decadence in Early Twentieth-Century Russian Art, "*Journal of Contemporary History* 17, no. 1, Decadence (January 1982): 95.

39. Ibid., 103. According to Bowlt, these artists included Isaak Brodsky, Fechin, and Boris Kustodiev.

40. "No doubt, therefore, the monsters of Anisfeld, the corpses and skeletons of Brodsky, the coffins of Fechin, the blood of Dobujinsky, etc. derived not only from a sense of civic indignation, but also from a more expressionistic, psychological urge, as was the case, for example, with Alfred Kubin's and Franz Kupka's contributions to *L'Assiette au Beurre* or with the many macabre and erotic illustrations for *Simplicissimus*." Ibid., 104.

41. Ibid., 105.

42. These qualities are evident in paintings throughout Fechin's career and in depictions of subjects as wide ranging as *Still Life with Oranges*, 1925 (p. 57), *Joe with Drum*, 1927–33 (p. 51), *Juan the Peon*, 1936 (p. 67), and *Seated Male Nude* (p. 47).

43. Sergei Bongart described the artist's process as follows:
"Fechin prepared his canvases himself. His canvases were extremely absorbent. He used oil paint almost without oil. He put the oil paint on an old newspaper and let it stand overnight. Most of the oil was absorbed by the paper. This left pigment with very little oil. Fechin mixed colors with lighter fluid or benzine or mineral spirits. He did this because of the flat, velvety effect; not a shiny finish. Because the canvas was absorbent, the treatment he used made the paint become hard very fast. For that reason he was able immediately to paint one coat on top of another which enabled the colors underneath to show thru (dry brush technique). Fechin's paintings cannot be varnished like regular oil paintings because if varnish is used the painting becomes gaudy and loses the principal charm and renders a flat, kind of tempera quality. Because Fechin did not varnish his oil paintings, he put them under glass to protect the painting. Because of his technique (painting without oil) paint loses its binder. Oil is the principal binder. For this reason the paint begins to peel from the canvas inasmuch as there is not enough binder inside."
(Bongart, *Fechin's Paintings*, typed document dated January 17, 1977, Frye Art Museum Archives.)

WAR AND REVOLUTION IN RUSSIA: 1914–1922

44. An article on duty on artworks in November 1914 noted that communication between Stimmel and Fechin was no longer possible.
"The presence in the present Tariff act of two provisions for "paintings in oil" requiring that they be proved originals has provoked a deal of friction between importers and the Government. A recent case came up for settlement Nov. 12 before the Board of General Appraisers when a protest by W. S. Stimmel, an insurance broker of Pittsburgh, was decided in favor of the importer. The painting in dispute is by Nicolas Fechin, and the importer claimed the artist lives in Russia, too far away to obtain his attestation. A witness was found familiar with the artist's work."
(*American Art News* 13, no. 7 [November 21, 1914]: 1.)

45. J. R. Hunter, statement, May 26, 1959 (copy dated June 20, 1975), 2, Archives of the Frye Art Museum.

46. The American Relief Administration was established in February 1919 to administer relief measures authorized by a congressional appropriation of $100 million. Russian relief was initiated in August 1921 under an agreement with the Soviet government, and by 1923, district missions were established in the capitals of most provinces of the Russian Socialist Federated Soviet Republic. During the worst period, nearly 11 million men, women, and children were fed. The relief administration's operations ended in Russia on June 15, 1923. See http://socialarchive.iath.virginia.edu/xtf/view?docId=american-relief-administration-russian-operations-cr.xml (accessed December 2012).

47. Around May 1922, William S. Stimmel purchased *Woman Who Smokes* for $500. The painting was shipped to the United States for the Annual Exhibition at the Carnegie Institute that year but did not arrive in time for the exhibition. Fechin used these funds to help pay passage for himself and his family to the United States. J. R. Hunter, statement, May 26, 1959 (copy dated June 20, 1975), 5, Archives of the Frye Art Museum.

48. J. R. Hunter states that Fechin arrived in September 1923 (ibid., 3-7); however, Fechin's autobiography states that he arrived in August. "On August 1, 1923 we first saw, through a thick fog, the fantastic skyline of New York": Nicolai Fechin, "Autobiography: The Russian Years," *Persimmon Hill* 8, no. 3 (1978): 17.

49. For *Lady in Pink*, no. 144, Gallery 61, see *Official Catalogue of the Department of Fine Arts, Panama-Pacific International Exposition* (San Francisco: The Wahlgreen Company, 1915), 100.

50. Eugen Neuhaus, *The Galleries of the Exposition: A Critical Review of the Paintings, Statuary and the Graphic Arts in the Palace of Fine Arts at the Panama-Pacific International Exposition* (San Francisco: Paul Elder and Company, 1915), 16, http://books.google.com/books?id=ZghDAAAAIAAJ&pg=PR1&lpg=PR1&dq=eugen+neuhaus+galleries+of+the+exposition+a+critical+review&source=bl&ots=utsAhnENW0&sig=xAHuIbY237r1MkVstyn_WVqb9sc&hl=en&sa=X&ei=jtv1UIysBaOyiQKX-oDIDA&ved=0CF8Q6AEwCA (accessed August 2012).

51. Christian Brinton, "International Arts at Pittsburgh," *International Studio* 46, no. 184 (June 1912): lxxxviii, xc.

52. Christian Brinton, "The Modern Spirit in Contemporary Painting," in *Impressions of the Art at the Panama-Pacific Exposition* (New York: John Lane Company, 1916), 12.

53. Ibid., 19.

54. *American Art News* 18, no. 5 (November 22, 1919): 2. The First Annual Exhibition of Contemporary International Art organized by the Dallas Art Association took place at the Adolphus Hotel in November 1919. In his foreword to the exhibition catalogue, Brinton described Fechin as an "academic realist." For *Lady in Pink*, no. 25 (illus.), and *Portrait of a Russian Actress*, no. 26, see *The First Annual Exhibition of Contemporary International Art* (Dallas: Dallas Art Association, 1919). The exhibition also included *Castle Hemsbach* by Wilhelm Trübner, on loan from Josef Stransky (illus.), now in the Frye Art Museum, and Franz von Stuck's *Listening Fauns*, on loan from Edward A. Faust.

55. For *Portrait of Abramotchiff* (Portrait of Abramichev), no. 105, Gallery N, see *The Catalogue of the Nineteenth Annual Exhibition at the Carnegie Institute, April 29 to June 30, 1920* (Pittsburgh, PA: Carnegie Institute, 1920). John R. Hunter is recognized in the catalogue's acknowledgments.

56. The painting was acquired by Hunter between 1911 and 1922. J. R. Hunter, statement, May 26, 1959 (copy dated June 20, 1975), 2, Archives of the Frye Art Museum.

57. Ibid., 5. Childs was in Russia with the American Relief Administration from 1921 to 1923. Overview of the J. Rives Childs Memoirs, Online Archive of California, http://www.oac.cdlib.org/findaid/ark:/13030/kt2w1031q1/ (accessed December 2012).

NEW YORK: 1923–1927

58. Nicolai Fechin, "Autobiography: The Russian Years," *Persimmon Hill* 8 no. 3 (1978): 17.

59. Aaron Harry Gorson had moved from Pittsburgh to New York in 1921. See http://www2009.ems.psu.edu/museum/Steidle/artists/Gorson.html (accessed December 2012).

60. J. R. Hunter, statement, May 26, 1959 (copy dated June 20, 1975), 7–8, Archives of the Frye Art Museum.

61. *The Art Institute of Chicago Special Exhibition Paintings by Nikolai Fechin* (Chicago: The Art Institute of Chicago, 1923). See J. R. Hunter, statement, May 26, 1959 (copy dated June 20, 1975), 9–10, Archives of the Frye Art Museum. Hunter notes that of the twenty-five paintings in the exhibition, Stimmel contributed eleven; Hunter, six; Childs, three; and Cowl and Balken, one each.

62. See "Futurism and After: David Burliuk, 1882–1967," Ukrainian Museum, http://ukrainianmuseum.org/burliuk/?q=node/1 (accessed December 2012).

63. See *American Art News* 21, no. 14 (January 13, 1923), 1–10.

64. *Exhibition of Russian Painting and Sculpture* (Brooklyn: The Brooklyn Museum, 1923).

65. Christian Brinton, introduction to ibid.

66. J. R. Hunter, statement, May 26, 1959 (copy dated June 20, 1975), 10, Archives of the Frye Art Museum. Brinton was paid a fee of $500 for preparing the catalogue.

67. Ibid., iv.

68. Ibid.

69. Ibid. The Moscow Art Theatre was renowned for its presentation of works by Tolstoy and Chekhov at the turn of the twentieth century.

70. *The Chief Thing*, by Nicolas Evreinoff (Nikolai Evreinov), translated by Leo Randole and Herman Bernstein, played at the Guild Theatre, New York, March 22–April 1926. It was directed by Philip Moeller and starred Edward G. Robinson (as "A Stage Director") and Lee Strasberg (as "A Prompter"). See http://www.imdb.com/name/nm0263810/otherworks (accessed December 2012).

71. Hayden Herrera, *Arshile Gorky: His Life and Work* (New York: Farrar, Straus & Giroux, 2003), 131.

72. "Current Exhibitions," *Bulletin of the City Art Museum of Saint Louis* 11, no. 184 (April 1926): 29.

TAOS AND CALIFORNIA: 1927–1955

73. "Taos Paintings by J. Young-Hunter," *Bulletin of the Minneapolis Institute of Arts* 9, no. 2 (February 1920): 16.

74. Mabel Dodge Luhan, *Lorenzo in Taos* (New York: Alfred A. Knopf, 1922), 3.

75. Keith L. Bryant, "The Atchison, Topeka and Santa Fe Railway and the Development of the Taos and Santa Fe Art Colonies," *Western Historical Quarterly* 9, no. 4 (October 1978): 442–43.

76. "Fechin Exhibit Opens Today," *Los Angeles Times*, April 1, 1928, C32.

77. Letter from Katherine Benepe Shackelford to Mary N. Balcomb. Mary N. Balcomb, *Nicolai Fechin* (Flagstaff: Northland Press, 1975), 124–6.

78. Fred Hogue, "Fechin—'The Tartar,'" *Los Angeles Times*, June 4, 1939, C7.

WORKS OF ART

a. Eugen Neuhaus, *The Galleries of the Exposition: A Critical Review of the Paintings, Statuary and the Graphic Arts in the Palace of Fine Arts at the Panama-Pacific International Exposition* (San Francisco: Paul Elder and Company, 1915), 16, http://books.google.com/books?id=ZghDAAAAIAAJ&pg=PR1&lpg=PR1&dq=eugen+neuhaus+galleries+of+the+exposition+a+critical+review&source=bl&ots=utsAhnENW0&sig=xAHuIbY237r1MkVstyn_WVqb9sc&hl=en&sa=X&ei=jtv1UIysBaOyiQKX-oDIDA&ved=0CF8Q6AEwCA (accessed August 2012).

b. Nicolai Fechin, "Autobiography: The Russian Years," *Persimmon Hill* 8, no. 3 (1978): 10.

c. James B. Townsend, "Annual Carnegie Institute Exhibition," *American Art News* 9, no. 29 (April 29, 1911): 4. It has not been possible to identify which child was portrayed.

d. *Special Exhibition Paintings by Nikolai Fechin, December 18, 1923 to January 20, 1924* (Chicago: The Art Institute of Chicago, 1923). Although the owner of the work was not indicated, it probably belonged to one of the American collectors William S. Stimmel, John R. Hunter, Clarkson Cowl, Edward Duff Balken, and J. Rives Childs.

e. Alexandra Fechin, *March of the Past* (Santa Fe, NM: Writers' Editions, 1937), 71, 72–73.

f. Nicolai Fechin, "Autobiography: The Russian Years." *Persimmon Hill* 8, no. 3 (1978): 15.

g. Alexandra Fechin, *March of the Past* (Santa Fe, NM: Writers' Editions, 1937), 134–35.

h. See Spencer Golub, *Evreinov: The Theatre of Paradox and Transformation* (Ann Arbor, MI: UMI Research Press, 1984), 153, https://journals.ku.edu/index.php/jdtc/article/viewFile/1765/1729 (accessed December 2012).

i. See Alexandra Smith, "Nikolai Evreinov and Edith Craig as Mediums of Modernist Sensibility," http://www.research.ed.ac.uk/portal/en/publications/nikolai-evreinov-and-edith-craig-as-mediums-of-modernist-sensibility(a461566f-9342-431a-a42f-afb33166fccc).html (accessed December 2012), and Francis M. Naumann and Gail Stavitsky, *Conversion to Modernism: The Early Work of Man Ray* (Montclair, NJ: The Montclair Art Museum, 2003), chapter 8, http://www.tfaoi.com/aa/4aa/4aa142.htm (accessed January 2013).

j. *Catalogue [of the] Twenty-Fourth Annual International Exhibition of Paintings, October 15–December 6, 1925* (Pittsburgh, PA: Carnegie Institute, 1925). See "Fechin Exhibit Opens Today," *Los Angeles Times,* April 1, 1928, C32: "Los Angeles people may remember his striking portrait of an artist wearing green earrings that was seen here three years ago in the foreign section of the Carnegie International Exhibition."

k. Frank Waters, *Of Time and Change* (Denver: MacMurray & Beck, 1998): 172.

l. James Karman, *The Collected Letters of Robinson Jeffers, with Selected Letters of Una Jeffers*, 2 (Stanford: Stanford University Press, 2011), 209.

m. Mabel Dodge Luhan, *Lorenzo in Taos* (Santa Fe: Sunstone Press, 2007), 116.

n. Arthur Hoeber, "The Winter Academy," *International Studio* 45, no. 180 (February 1912): xcii.

o. "Nana of Taos," Art, *Los Angeles Times*, February 9, 1930, F5.

p. Fred Hogue, "Fechin the Tartar," *Los Angeles Times*, February 25, 1930, A4.

q. J. R. Hunter, statement, May 26, 1959 (copy dated June 20, 1975), Archives of the Frye Art Museum.

r. Eya Fechin Branham, foreword to Mary N. Blacomb, *Nicolai Fechin* (Flagstaff, AZ: Northland Press, 1975), xviii.

s. Fred Hogue, "Fechin—'The Tartar,'" *Los Angeles Times*, June 4, 1939, C7.

t. *Lorena Lloyd Montgomery Paintings, Caroline A. Lloyd Sculpture*, May 19–31, 1941, Stendahl Galleries; A.M., "Sisters Nearing Twilight of Life Display Works," *Los Angeles Times*, May 25, 1941, C8.

This catalogue is published on the occasion of the exhibition *Nicolai Fechin* at the Frye Art Museum, Seattle, from February 9 to May 19, 2013.

Nicolai Fechin is organized by the Foundation for International Arts and Education, Bethesda, Maryland; the Frye Art Museum, Seattle, Washington; and the State Museum and Exhibition Center ROSIZO under the auspices of the Ministry of Culture of the Russian Federation.

The exhibition is curated by Jo-Anne Birnie Danzker and funded by the Frye Foundation with the generous support of Frye Art Museum members and donors. It is sponsored by BNY Mellon Wealth Management and the Filatov Family Art Foundation. Seasonal support is provided by 4Culture, Seattle Office of Arts & Cultural Affairs, Canonicus Fund, and ArtsFund.

The catalogue is published by the Frye Art Museum with the support of BNY Mellon Wealth Management and the Filatov Family Art Foundation.

Frye Art Museum Board of Trustees
David Buck, President
Douglas Adkins
Jan Hendrickson
Kate Janeway
Frank P. Stagen

Jo-Anne Birnie Danzker, Director

Exhibition
Curator: Jo-Anne Birnie Danzker
Exhibition Coordinator: Amelia Hooning
Research Assistant: Lauren Palmor
Collections Manager/Registrar: Cory Gooch
Collections Assistant: Jess Atkinson
Exhibition Design: Shane Montgomery
Exhibition Preparation: Mark Eddington, Benjamin Eisman, Ken Kelly, Elizabeth Mauro, John Shimer, and Paula Sweet

Catalogue
Editor: Jo-Anne Birnie Danzker
Publication Coordinator: Amelia Hooning
Research Assistant: Lauren Palmor
Collections Research: Cory Gooch and Jess Atkinson
Copy Editor: Laura Iwasaki
Proofreader: Roberta Klarreich
Photography (Frye Collection): Spike Mafford

Design: Victoria Culver

Printed in Seattle by Printing Control
Color and print management by icolor, Seattle

Cover: Nicolai Fechin. *Lady in Pink (Portrait of Natalia Podbelskaya)* (detail), 1912. Oil on canvas. 45 1/2 x 35 in. (115.57 x 88.9 cm). Frye Art Museum, 1990.005.

Copyright © 2013 by the Frye Art Museum and the authors.

All rights reserved. No part of this publication may be reproduced, stored, or transmitted in any form or by any means, electronic or mechanical, without permission in writing from the Frye Art Museum.

The Frye Art Museum has diligently endeavored to research and identify all copyright holders for the material appearing in this book. For questions regarding copyright of illustrations, please contact the Frye Art Museum.

ISBN: 978-0-9889495-0-8

Frye Art Museum
704 Terry Ave.
Seattle, WA 98104
USA
www.fryemuseum.org